LEAVING MY FOOTPRINTS ON THE TRAVELLER'S TRAIL

DISCOVERING MY PASSION

STUTHI AITHAL

Made with ♥ on the Notion Press Platform
www.notionpress.com

A memoir of my travels but a dedication to my ever-supportive father for allowing me to see the world in a different, unique yet enjoyable and memorable manner
Thank you Appa!

Contents

1

Welcome Aboard, Reader!

♡

Travel brings books alive. Seeing the Himalayas roll past my window, wearing snow capes and pine suits is an experience worth wondering about. The tumbleweeds wave a feisty hello to me when I sail aboard a cruise on the Thar Desert's sand dunes! The cool raindrops give a friendly hug whenever I visit my leafy friends in the Northeast. The sea embraces my knees as I stand on the beach feeling the cool air on my cheeks enjoying the delight of being in my birthplace – the seaside.

I personally feel my favourite books come alive when I visit those places. Seeing nature cast its spell on you and feeling the author in you spring to reality is indeed a pleasure. Besides being an avid reader, I love to explore India from the eyes of a car or a train or even a plane! The illuminated peepers of these vehicles tell me the story of the cities from their 'honk' of view. The windscreen tells me its woes of battling against the varying weather. But my eyes tell me a different story in all, one of books springing to life, of trees talking about the town's top news and rivers posting letters across banks.

Travelling is a passion that I have been pursuing for the past many years. It helps me broaden my perspective towards life. Seeing the diversity of my nation has instilled an emotion of respect and love for my country. Collecting memories of different lands has indeed been an exhilarating experience. Feeling the varied yet united soils of India unite in my heart is a sensation to cherish.

I am an accomplished traveller, I feel, for I have travelled the world all within my own country. My friend, reading this introduction, you might be wondering why did I say so? I have seen the breezy Sahara in the Thar, the chilling Alps in the Himalayas, the humid Amazon rainforest in the Northeast and of course, the peachy Hawaiian beaches along the Malabar Coast!

Trekking has always been a getaway for me from the busy schedule of school and studies! I have forever been open to being out in the wild and bush, feeling the warmth of Mother Nature embrace me. It is not a sport for me but an emotion, indeed. Rambling through the thickest of the thicket, the trees showering colourful florets on the leafy trail is a grand welcome, don't you agree, my good reader? Sensing the lush green grass squish under my boots, the dry twigs crack under my feet and seeing the pugmarks of my fellow kinsfolk on the path is an adventurous and exciting encounter. These amazing treks have a special place in my heart as I have spent the best time of my life with my family during these holidays.

Folks like you, are kind enough to read through this long introduction but on turning the next few pages you will be so hooked, that even the most bored cat on the hearthrug will jump up to catch your attention. Why's that so, you ask? Ha-ha! For you have in front of you, the garnered collection of *my* travels, procured from secret journals and diaries excavated from the mustiest corners of ... *obviously* my folder! This assortment of varied voyages is an enjoyable read so go ahead and lose yourself in the nooks and crannies of my country!

2

Exploring Every trekker's dream

I still clearly remember the first day of this beautiful experience of seeing a new side of Himalayan trekking, one that was raw, untouched, and serene. These words are an understatement to the exquisiteness of the Nepali Himalayas. Seeing the verdant hills roll past, to gazing at the mighty Annapurna Range, this entire encounter was utter bliss. Never have I ever seen such stunningly eroded cliffs; they appeared as though someone had carved them by hand, just for me to see. The feeling of living in a teahouse in Nepal is unforgettable. For the first time, I saw an oxymoron in nature flourish in front of my very own eyes: the dry, windy, and gravelled knolls flaunted their elegance to one side, while on the other, the lush green coniferous woods flashed their grace. Ah! Those two weeks of spending our time with nature and experiencing the Nepali culture were fun, rejuvenating, and a delight to the eyes. And yes! This trek does hold a special place in my heart for it is the first time my father and I went on a trek, just the both of us, father and daughter.

My mind can never forget the delight of sipping black tea, alongside a roaring waterfall that bowed a polite *namaste* to us as we drove to the quaint village of Chame. The long hours of trekking through the steep paths and chilling winds sure did make us exhausted but the tranquil scenery around soothed our aching limbs and urged us on to our destination. It was on this trek that I was truly able to understand the exceptional inspiration that Mother Nature gives us to achieve our goals and keep moving despite all difficulties. The first day of the trek was absolute pleasure, seeing the massive Annapurna II rise and tower over you, humbling one as they trudged along, enveloped by the oxymoron of nature. The view from the Upper Pisang Monastery was simply breath-taking, marking an unforgettable start to the journey.

The evenings spent in the sweet teahouses were pleasant, listening to the guitar being strummed to melodious numbers by Ajit uncle, listening to intriguing incidents from Romil sir's vast climbing experience, laughing at Ajit uncle's jokes and riddles or happily playing games around the warm *Bukhari*. It was here that I understood the true meaning of 'triumph' and 'will power'. The joy of accomplishing your goal despite your limbs screaming for retreat is immeasurable. I was able to experience this ultimate bliss on the first summit push to the Ice Lake at 15,200 feet, supported encouragingly by Amit uncle and Harroop didi. The crystal-clear lake was a feast to the eyes. The pain in our limbs from the climb got washed away the next morning, seeing the Annapurna Range glisten in the early morning sun. I clearly remember the sheer happiness in my eyes while on the trail as we could see the regal

Annapurna and the snowy Tilicho mountains, appearing as though they were just a stone's throw away. The most memorable evening of this entire trek was spent playing 'Taboo' and 'Dumb-charades' in the cosy, colourful teahouse of Shree Kharkha. The mesmerising view of the hills dropping down to the quaint river flowing merrily in the scenery was in the background. En route to the Tilicho Base Camp my heart skipped many a beat as we squeezed through the narrow, treacherous path traversing through the head of a Tyrannosaurus Rex (the rocks were eroded in such a way that my active imagination kicked into action) and tiptoeing across his back. Deepa aunty and Revathi aunty were extremely caring and helpful throughout this trek. An icy brook gushed alongside our teahouse, and so our amazing trek leader, Romil Sir, took us there on a relaxing numb-feet therapy. It was very enjoyable for the clouds had decided to take the rest of the afternoon off, so we could see the grand Tilicho mountain loom over us, dressed in a frosty shirt and black trousers. But ahoy there, my friend! The scenery hasn't hit the hay yet. The pristine and impeccable Tilicho lake at 16,200 feet was truly worth the bumpy horse ride (Wondering why? Well, I had fallen sick the previous night and thus had to go on horseback, sad but a different exciting encounter). The day seemed to be trying various tricks to please me that day! It started out clear and sunny, but the clouds were back from their leave earlier that day and enveloped us in a blinding fog. But soon a ray of light shone through the mist and the weather cleared. As we all devoured the view of the Tilicho Lake, we heard an avalanche roar its arrival on the one of the surrounding mountains and our hearts jumped up in part excitement and part fear on hearing an avalanche for the first time. In short, it was an exhausting but delightful day, one that I shall forever cherish.

Trekking out there in the wilderness, I was able to appreciate and admire nature. The swift change of landscape from leafy forests to barren clifftops, and then suddenly to slippery trails carving their way through the scrublands, was a moving picture of true beauty. This was the real reminder of nature's creations. Ah! The day of the summit push to the Thorang La Pass was exhilarating. The spine-tingling joy of waking up before the rooster crowed and forging our way through the mist and slight snow, before finally setting foot on the 17,872 feet high pass was beyond measure. The view of the surrounding mountains was speechless. My jaw dropped open as I turned around to see a panorama of Himalayas, their mighty peaks glimmering in the early morning sun. The cherry on the cake were the clouds, sparkling a pristine azure to a clear white in a smooth gradient, a few spots of yellow bringing on the sunshine to the mesmerising vista. It appeared as though the greatest artist of all time: nature, had painted the canvas of the sky in such delightful hues just to please us and applaud our efforts.

I have realised, being on quite a few treks, that the days may be long and tiring but the landscape around and our co-trekkers make it a memory that you will never forget, be it the first day or that of the summit push each member and every view make it count. On this trek, each trekker starred as an excellent actor in this unforgettable trip. Anita aunty never made me feel alone or miss my mother while Ajit uncle became a dear friend of mine, cracking jokes to inspirit me and telling me about the many places he has visited across the globe. He had such vast ken on a wide variety of subjects that I was impressed and inspired to be someone like him. The greatest joy for me was the interaction between an author-in-the-making (me) and an experienced writer (Ajit uncle). It was a delight to meet someone like Harroop didi who was forever upbeat and raring to go. She was a true go-getter, enthusing me to become the best version of myself. Deepa aunty and Shilpa aunty were very sweet, always encouraging and praising me with heartfelt words, their resilience and determination was motivating. And I enjoyed the company of Divya didi too, whose delicious pickles always reminded me of my grandmother's home. Oh yes! How could I even forget Romil sir, the one who pushed us all on and made this trek a humongous success! He was an amazing, brilliant and galvanising trek leader. He was always full of thrilling tales ranging from his Everest climb to that of Mt. Kilimanjaro to Friendship Peak and many more which raised one's goosebumps so high that they are on the verge of jetting off your skin. His relentless energy and support was what spurred me on towards the destination every day. Rita aunty was the star of the trek. Every day, she would give us a smile and a thumbs up whenever we came across her. She proved that - 'Trekking is not a sport but an emotion, the true believers of which shall forever pursue it irrespective of their age or strength, for all that matters is will power'. Revathi aunty and Vedavati aunty showered me with a lot of care and love. Their presence in the trek made it special for me, because very seldom do you ever find people on a trek who speak your mother tongue. And last but not the least, Aarav bhaiya was the sportiest and most energetic person on the trek leading the way with our guide. A grateful vote of thanks to Team Boots and Crampons, along with all the guides and porters who made this trek a memorable experience.

Our trek didn't stop there! I clearly remember the peace I felt at the Muktinath Mandir, the cold zephyr brushing away our fatigue. We were now off to the most happening place in Nepal, can you guess that, my dear reader? Psst... It's Pokhara! It was a beautiful place. Lively colourful markets, skirting the banks of a lake so large that the opposite bank appeared to be a toy set. The fairy lights dancing around each shop entrance reminded me of Diwali in India. The evening my father and I spent around the captivating Phewa lake, strolling and enjoying Nepali momos was a rejuvenating experience. The ginormous Shiva statue at Pokhara was devotional. The highlight for me for the entire stay in Pokhara was the Gupteshwar Mahadev Cave which was deep down in a dark cave that at certain places, my blood ran cold if even a drop of water dripped onto my shirt, also the roof was so low at places that I had to stoop and go. But the glowing waterfall there stole my heart. It was awesome. The Everest Museum too was a wonder amongst the many museums I have visited, making the entire stay in Pokhara very enjoyable.

Like all films, this movie too had its ending, one where all the actors came together and thanked each other for one another's dauntless support and the director felicitated and appreciated everyone's effort. Sorry my dear reader, if I am being too ambiguous; but you see, it was a true delight to be treated so regally throughout the trek and the farewell is the grandest you can ever imagine and the cherry on the cake being the moving de-briefing. It was an opportunity for all of us to applaud each other's efforts and congratulate oneself on being able to complete the trek with flying colours. Romil sir's words of praise are forever entrenched in my heart which I shall forever remember and recount. The many mementos we were given that evening will always remind me of this trek, its wonderful trekkers and of course, the Nepali spirit of trekking.

These two weeks of ultimate pleasure in the wild accompanied by our very own Indian Bear Grylls (Romil sir) were like a flipbook, the pages flew by and the days of camaraderie were being scripted in my memory. This trek has given me so many new experiences, that of flying international for the first time, of meeting so many people from different walks of life, and of course of trekking in Nepal surrounded by varying landscape. Each stride, every victory was not only a result of my strength but also of my will power, the power of which I was able to realise, clear and true, on this trek. Not to forget, this trek was also a success because of the immensely supportive and lively team that I had the company of, all throughout the trek. This trek has shown me a better, stronger, resolved and more confident version of myself and made me realise my true potential to improve. Every faltering moment, I looked up and ahead and thought of the joy I would experience on reaching the teahouse among the first few there. I realised that being on a trek was happiness, but its true joy lay in the landscape all around and enjoying the real beauty of nature.

Trekking is seeing life – raw, untouched and so immaculately beautified by nature in a way, that even our eyes feel the exquisiteness of Mother Nature seep into them and providing every exhausted limb an energy boost like never before. It was nothing short of an adventure of exploring the undiscovered. Embracing trekking has been a life-changing experience for me but coming on this trek has given a new twist in my saga of hiking in the wild.

3

Seeing the colours of Rajasthan come alive

My muscles were taut as I hopped from one foot to the other atop the platform, expecting the arrival of our train to Jaipur.

My mind is replaying the events of the past eleven days as I rest my fingers on my chin; deep in thought. I picture the sparkle of excitement in my eyes as we boarded the train, the chuckles of delight as I allowed the sand of the Thar to swallow my feet, the pride in my heart as I witnessed the Indo-Pak border and what not!

I was so involved with my academics and co-curricular activities that I didn't have time to put my feet up! This winter vacation, as I really needed some time off, my father decided to take us to the tourist hub of India: Rajasthan!

On our first day in Jaipur, we were blown away by the intricate architecture of the Hawa Mahal. Its beautiful windows with shards of tinted glass were throwing colourful beams of sunlight. The Jantar Mantar amazed me a lot as I had never imagined that the kings of those times had made blueprints and test models before building the final astronomical marvel. I smile to myself as I recall the joy bubbling in me as I enjoyed myself thoroughly at the legendary restaurant – 'Chokhi Dhani'. My most memorable moment at Chokhi Dhani was when, at the magic show the magician pulled a marvelous trick on me. He shook my jeans and unbelievably coins tinkled out!

Our tour carried on to the largest museum I have ever been to – 'The Albert Museum'! So large, so unique a museum I had never seen. Interestingly, it had a large variety of coins, carpets, frescoes, blue pottery, lacquer work and what not! I was astonished to hear that Raja Man Singh, the king who had built the Amer Fort, had twelve wives and had built separate apartments for each. The beautiful Jal Mahal, astoundingly, has two storeys underwater, and one above water. This palace was surrounded by such serenity that I wished to never go away from it.

The best part of the entire stay in Jaipur was the visit to the handmade paper factory. We saw the entire process of making handmade paper: from chopping the cotton rags into fine pieces to settling and drying it to the last step of finally packaging it. I even liked our visit to the Block Printing Unit where the employees printed metres of cloth in minutes in front of our very own eyes. I remember the moment as my mouth flew open in surprise that day as I saw the Jaivan Cannon: the world's largest cannon, loom in front of me as I climbed up the steps at the Jaigarh Fort! It was so ginormous, that my eyes had to pop out of their sockets to observe the cannon completely. The day ended pleasantly with the mesmerising view atop the Nahargarh Fort. One can see the whole of the Pink City from the fort's terrace.

I was delighted that after a long time the entire family was sharing each other's joys and enjoying together. Ah! How can I forget the day in Bapu Bazaar where I shopped *keychains* till I dropped! I can't stifle my laughter as I re-imagine the moment where my mother was staring open-mouthed at me as I bent down and bought eleven keychains from a little stall. The surprised look on her face and my father's smile is a moment I'll never forget.

The next place on our holiday plan was Jodhpur. The most exciting part of our stay in Jodhpur was that we were staying at the house of the descendant of the Maharaja of Jodhpur, himself! The breezy balcony was quite special for the boughs of the adjacent tree used to harbour a variety of arboreal animals that would always perk me up. I liked the Ghanta Ghar, for the market around it and the vintage feel around the clocktower itself made me feel as though I had been transported back in time! The Mandore Garden was pleasant as we whiled away our time in the Adventure Zone and Music Arena. The greenery all around the garden made me feel as calm as the sea with the cool wind stroking my cheeks and relaxing me.

Can you even imagine the thought of a museum having a variety of antique clocks, some shaped like chests and others were inlaid in stunning statues? This marvellous museum at Umaid Bhawan Palace fascinated me the most! The Jaswant Thada was a tranquil place with mighty marble carvings and structures all around. I couldn't believe my ears when I heard that this beautiful place was the final resting place of the Rajput kings of that time! But whatever be it, the Jaswant Thada gave such a fabulous royal ambiance that I feel words are too less to describe my feelings. The Mehrangarh Fort was very picturesque, and I liked the entire time I spent touring this fort. The magnificent view of the Blue City from the fort was so delightful that I felt our regal stay in Jodhpur had been given a worthy ending!

Next up on our tour list was the Golden City: Jaisalmer! Even the entire drive to Jaisalmer was so beautiful, with small shrubs with cotton-like flowers popping in here and there, and the sand dunes rolling calmly across as far as the eye could see! Surprisingly, we saw a lot of windmills, rotating away merrily, generating kilowatts of electricity within moments. The spookiest place I have ever been to: Kuldhara, was so scary that it frightened the daylights out of me, even in the afternoon! I still giggle as I recall the moment I was completely alarmed as an empty packet of chips rustled behind me due to the wind. Frankly, I was relieved when we left the 'haunted' village. The most enjoyable evening of the entire trip was in Jaisalmer; at the desert camp on New Year's Eve where we went to the nearby sand dunes atop camels. The joy was immeasurable as I felt the sand give way beneath my shoes. I remember the sweet Rajasthani songs being sung by the artists at the camp. It was indeed an invigorating jumpstart to the year.

The following day, my breath was taken away by the intense atmosphere around the powerful Tanot Mata Mandir, full of devotion with many followers seeking the blessings of the goddess. The most intriguing part about the temple was that during the 1965 Pakistani attack the formidable ambiance of the goddess had protected the area from 3000 shells, some of the unexploded ones were still on display in the premises. We prayed to Her to shower Her bountiful blessings unto us. That day I added another feather to my hat with the Indo-Pak border in Punjab being the first, Indo-China border being the second and now the Indo-Pak border being the third. My chest was bursting with pride as I witnessed the tight security on the border! There was an increased respect in me for our Indian soldiers who patrol the borders day and night during the visit to the Jaisalmer War Memorial themed on the Battle of Longewala.

The stay was given a boost, with living *in* the Jaisalmer Fort surrounded by its vibrant markets. I loved the Patwa Haveli, its beautiful carvings in the famous golden sandstone of Jaisalmer, sunlight sparkling at the mirrors decorated on the first floor. I can't help recalling the time we had spent purchasing items at a huge wholesale shop. My mother and I couldn't stop ourselves and, finally ended up buying two bags full of merchandise. The icing on the cake for me, as a foodie, for the entire trip was the delicious Rajasthani cuisine we ate - kachoris, *gatta* curry, *ker sangri, kadhi, sev tamatar* and the list goes on and on. My mouth still waters as I imagine the steaming dishes arriving in front of me.

The last place on our travel itinerary was the holy city of Pushkar. The most intriguing part of our stay at the hotel was the dressing sense of the manager! The very evening, we checked in, my mother and I were laughing our heads off as I proposed the idea of him being the great-great-grandson of the master detective Sherlock Holmes, for his hat, his muffler wrapped around his neck, his tweed coat and his sharp features.

The spellbinding Brahma temple with the name of all the followers inscribed on the walls and the floor of the temple shall always be imprinted in my mind. The power of piety of devotees could be felt to the core in the Brahma Temple. The crystal clear Pushkar Lake was a sight to behold, with crimson rose petals floating all around. The pristine blue paired with the contrasting red was a painting come to life. The light and sound show about Rajasthan at the Gadisar Lake was an experience that I will never forget! Adding to the memories was the visit to the Savitri Mata Mandir, located atop a steep hill. The ropeway that took us to the temple gave spellbinding views of the entire Pushkar City. We sought the blessings of the goddess. The *langurs* prancing around the mandir were very gentle and even took roasted gram from my very own hands!

If I picture the whole of Rajasthan as a book, then it is such that I can ever keep it down. Each page tells a tale of its own. As I turn each leaf, I realize that Rajasthan is not the arid land that everyone thinks it to be, it also has a lush green side, with Banswsari & Pushkar. But, the Thar of Rajasthan has its own splendour with cities like Jaisalmer & Bikaner. Rajasthan is not just a magnificent state but a heaven for those who love to travel and explore new places, from far and near. It is a place full of exotic and diverse culture, tradition, clothing, cuisine and the list goes on. This trip to Rajasthan had indeed been a wonderful experience, with me exploring the various cities that Rajasthan is so famous for! We, as proud Indians should embrace this diversity with open arms. I believe that to travel is to see the life around us, experience it from the eyes of others whom we meet and interact with.

This trip has ticked several locations off my travel bucket list. I hope that the next time I come to Rajasthan I will be able to witness its exquisiteness with another outlook.

4
Off to the Richest Princely State of British India: Mysuru

As I watched the Chamundi Hills approach in the horizon, rumbling closer and closer as our car neared the foothills of this range, I realized the diversity of the landscape in India; ranging from the shrubbery and cacti of Rajasthan in the West, and dense and humid rainforests of Sikkim in the East to the pine and fir forests in Uttarakhand located in North India to at last the sparsely distributed deciduous forests of Mysuru in South India. It is a delight to be able to relish the geographical beauty of our country in person!

Finally, the annual examinations were over, and I could not stop fidgeting until the day our flight bound for Bengaluru took off. It had been over a year since my last visit to my maternal grandparents' house in January 2023. My joy on being able to spend nine days with my dear grandparents knew no bounds. After spending a few days with them we all set off for a trip to Mysuru. It was an amazing experience to see the steep hills and bushy trees scuttle in to make some space in my mind's eye. On the way to the majestic city of Mysuru we visited the famous town, once ruled by Tipu Sultan, which was by the name Srirangapatna. There we saw a small area with a board indicating that the body of 'The Tiger of Mysuru': Tipu Sultanhad been found there. A few hundred metres ahead were the frightening dungeons of the fort. The blocks of cement used to chain the prisoners that were still existing scared the daylights out of me! Soon we left the place and headed to the beautiful temple located in the premises of this grand fortress. As I walked on the holy ground my mouth fell open on hearing that the temple is from the times of the ancient kings and is still as strong and stable as ever. After seeking the blessings of the Lord, we mounted our car to go to the world-famous bird sanctuary near Mysuru. As our driver parked the car in the parking lot, we were able to hear the distant cackling and calls of the birds in Ranganathittu Bird Sanctuary. As we roamed around in the spacious enclosure we came across a view point where we were able to see the various birds gliding over the surface of the lake trying to find a suitable fish to fill their bellies for the afternoon. We saw many birds gliding to the tree adjacent to the viewpoint and trying hard to pluck twigs and branches to make a comfortable nest for them to live in. After enjoying the squawking and gurgling of the water birds to our heart's content we continued our journey to our destination: Mysuru! As we weaved our way through the traffic to finally reach our hotel I was surprised to see an elaborate statue of different kings at every intersection in the city. After a filling lunch and ample rest, we left for the famous 'Jaganmohan Art Gallery'. There we saw various paintings of court-scenes, the famous Dussehra

Yatra and many portraits of the diverse kings who ruled over Mysuru. My personal favourite of the paintings was the one in which a king of the Wadiyar dynasty stood alongside his pet dog. The security guard there showed us how the dog appeared to be looking only at us no matter from which direction we look at it! It surprised me as I wondered the genius artists of the time must have worked on the paintings for so long to present such an illusion. I held my breath as I saw some of the most stunning pieces of art painted by Raja Ravi Varma. After satisfying our artistic desires, we exited the Art Gallery and embarked on a drive to the must-visit KRS Dam in Mysuru. It was full of picturesque fountains. Later in the evening at KRS Dam, we saw a mesmerizing musical fountain show, the location of which we travelled to via a motorboat in the backwaters of the dam! At the show, the water sprung up and down, left and right and in all other unimaginable angles. The movement of the water in synchronization with the music and lights was indeed an experience one must cherish in their lifetime. Soon after the show, we walked back to the entrance while admiring the lights sparkling on the surface of the Cauvery River. Then, the sound of rumbling stomachs filled the air thus we went to the restaurant at the top of the bucket-list of all who wish to visit Mysuru that is the 'Vinayaka Mylari Dose'! We thoroughly enjoyed the *dosas*. We had come all the way to Mysuru and did not have a cup of its popular *kappi* (filter coffee) then we would do injustice to its rich culture and cuisine! Hence, my parents and grandparents had a cup of filter coffee each while I enjoyed some steaming hot lemon tea.

The following morning, after a restful sleep filled with fascinating dreams about magical paintings I woke up to a refreshing morning. After a quick breakfast we went to the great, grand Mysuru Palace. We saw impressive hallways encrusted with 24 karat gold, huge durbars, imposing ivory doors and what not! The last durbar was the grandest with bright paints and gold plating glistening everywhere. As we stepped down we saw a silver door through which the king used to enter. We even saw the elegant wedding hall of the kings who once ruled Mysuru. The entire Mysuru Palace was exquisite!

Soon we checked out from our hotel and drove all the way to Channapatna. The route was dotted with beautiful ivory wood trees with leaves glistening in the mid-morning sun. Upon reaching the quaint little town we saw several shops selling toys and other such delightful souvenirs, all carved out of wood. I purchased the famous Channapatna doll pair with had been painted in vibrant hues which brought it to life! We also bought a beautiful *diya* stand to place it in front of our *mandir* at home.

Mysuru – a city that continues to astound historians, tourists, and locals alike with its diverse culture, tradition, and history. The stunning shades of brown and green that paint the scenery of Mysuru distinguish it from the forested areas of the North and the Northeast; and the aridity in the West. It is a city that stands with its head held high with plush culture and traditions as feathers in its hat. It has a rich history, embedded with one of the most chivalrous kings battling against the British to maintain the dignity and unity of their kingdoms. The vibrant colours that beautify the names of all the gallant soldiers and rulers in the pages of the history of Mysuru shall last forever, never fading in the hearts of all proud Indians. We, the people of India, shall always appreciate, applaud, and uphold the religious, social, and traditional diversity and integrity of our nation.

5

Setting foot on the World's Crown

"Woohoo!" I hollered in joy as we stood in line for the immigration at the airport. It was my first-ever international trip! Hold your horses tight, my dear reader! You must be wondering where I was off to? Any guesses... Oh yes, I was bound on a trip to Nepal! How amazing is that!

After two months of steaming in the heat of Lucknow, I was finally flying to my dream destination, knocking another location off my list, Kathmandu. The immense joy pumping through my blood as I saw my passport getting its first stamp was immeasurable. The glimpse of the Himalayas from the aeroplane's window was awesome. That evening we roamed around the hotspot of Kathmandu – Thamel. There were trillions of colourful shops selling trekking gear, souvenirs, relics and trekking gear again. My good friend! In the tongue of a true Lucknowite Thamel was like the Aminabad of Kathmandu only a bit more happening and a ton more pretty. There were many shops selling beautiful paintings mainly featuring intricate mandalas.

The market was a source of excitement every evening as we explored different dimensions and streets leading out from it.

The devotional visit to the world-renowned Pashupatinath Temple is forever ingrained in my heart. I prayed whole heartedly to the Lord to bless my family and I with His bountiful blessings. Driving through the smooth roads, watching life blossom in the merry city, we came across many a temple and stupa. I was astonished to know that each stroke of the brush on the Boudhanath Stupa had its very own significance, pertaining to not only Buddhism but also on emotional and social values in our daily life. The first glimpse of this stupa held me rooted to the spot for a few moments. The spell-binding Durbar Square had so many vintage buildings made out of wood and bricks without a speck of cement, they took me back in time, one where mighty kings roamed these very palaces and the Living Goddess (the Kumari) blessed the people of Nepal with her presence. Ah! It was mesmerising. The day earnt an unnatural twist, read on my good friend to know what happened. I still can't push the queer incident at the Swayambhu Gompa to the back of my grey matter. You must be imagining some gruesome incident, aren't you? But no, the presence of ... monkeys everywhere, from the parapet to the bench, dangling along the railings, they were all over the place. It was nice but a bit petrifying, for you never know, when you might have to turn into a cap-seller battling against a monkey for your chips and Frooti or your mobile phone! Nevertheless, the joy of flicking a coin into a wishing pond is immeasurable and I was able to experience it at this elegant Stupa. The holiest festival in Nepal is Buddha Purnima and we were able to experience the colourful processions in front of our eyes, hundreds of girls and boys singing in cheerful voices, men and women dressed elegantly in the traditional Nepali attire carrying the statues of the Lord and singing His praises. This delightful scene was visible from the intricately carved wooden mesh windows of the palace in the Patan Durbar Square while we were traversing through it. The original plaster used in the construction of the building was still intact, making me marvel at the advancement in construction back in those times, such that the mortar has lasted so long that I was able to see it in perfect condition although slightly yellowed due to immense age. I was surprised to know that even the shape of a temple depended on a couple of factors, as in the Krishna Temple there which was octagonal in shape because Lord Krishna is the eighth incarnation of Lord Vishnu. But the day doesn't hit the hay here! The amazing Chandragiri Cable Car was the best, highest, and the most exhilarating one I have ever been to. The view was ultimate, it beat all the ropeways I have ever been to. Those fifteen minutes in the cable car were the best in my life, always to be cherished with chuckles of joy. Unfortunately, the clouds had decided to welcome us with a soft hug, blocking our view of the mountains all around. But nevertheless, the slight breeze and cloudy sky made it a beautiful memory. The days spent in Kathmandu were full of fun, shopping and family time. We three together spent the time of our lives enjoying the Thamel market, the three Durbar Squares and all the scenic locations we visited. It was a delightful and intriguing experience at the Bhaktapur Durbar Square which had many temples dedicated to various gods and goddesses, I liked the concept of showing God as the strongest through hierarchical statues bordering the steep staircase to the central hall. The temples comprised of intricately carved brass entrances and brightly coloured elaborate doors. It was a good encounter that is inscribed in my memory. Oh my! How could I even forget the picturesque drive up the winding roads to the mesmerizingly tall Kailash Mahadev statue. We could catch a glimpse of Kathmandu from about every single hairpin bend and the view was breath-taking! We marvelled the view from the top, worshipped the deity and then made our way to a location, seeing which my eyes nearly popped out of their sockets. It was the Hanging Bridge! It swayed over a gushing river surrounded by a scrubby ravine, ooh! It was terrifying but exhilarating. The cool breeze and the sparse sunshine made the experience refreshing halfway through the bridge, but suddenly out of the green (for there was lush greenery all around) rain started coming down in buckets, giving us a thorough shower. Ah! It was a marvellous crossing. I do remember the incredible view that my eyes captured atop the view tower at Nagarkot, the sun bidding us farewell for the day as he hid himself under the quilt of the Kathmandu Valley and the dusk zephyr whistling a soft lullaby to the Sun.

That was just about it, an eloquent expression of my dream trip. It was nothing short of a quest of discovering the unexplored. Kathmandu is a true paradise whose beauty is yet to be reconnoitred. This trip to Nepal was a true treat to the eyes, from exciting night markets in Thamel to ancient stupas and temples like the Swayambhu Stupa and the Pashupatinath Mandir. The days were always full of fun, sightseeing and fun again! It is a memory I shall forever cherish.

Every day, I wished the evening would never set in and we

could keep enjoying the beauty of Kathmandu through the night.

> ***A family adventure is nothing short of a vivid memoir of love, joy and togetherness, come to life as a privilege that I often enjoy and treasure.***

6

A Peek into my Beautiful Hometown

My heart flutters with joy each time I hear the familiar hum as the aeroplane takes off the runway on its onward journey to my most favourite destination; Bengaluru: a city crowning everyone's travel bucket list, they believe that a trip pan-India is incomplete without a visit to the nation's IT hub but for me it holds a homely feeling in my heart – one of an abode of love, of comfort, of mischievous pranks and of course, a warm hug to look forward to, each time I visit my dear hometown. Having been there every year to visit my dearest grandparents, the garden city of India has stamped its mark on my memory as a place I connect to not only socially but also emotionally. International tourists regard a trip to the Silicon Valley as a checkbox ticked on their tour list, but this city attracts me personally. I feel as though the city itself calls me, "Hey Stuthi! Come, take a tour of the place you were born in."

This city is full of so many spots worth a click and a gape! The Vidhana Soudha, Cubbon park, Bannerghatta national park, Jawaharlal Nehru planetarium, the Visvesvaraya museum. I cannot stop wondering if the best tourist spots in India for academicians and nature lovers is here apart from the northeast and the Himalayas! It appears Karnataka is not a part of India instead it feels as though it is the other way around. One can see the breezy hills of the Western Ghats and experience its beauty in Savandurga and the lush Arabica and Robusta coffee plantations in Coorg. We can experience the fun at the beach in Mangalore, that too all these dreamy offbeat locations are just a few hours away from Bengaluru. It is such a delight to get away from busy life by just hopping into the car and manoeuvring it to our desired weekend getaway!

In the pleasant evenings of Bengaluru, it seems as though the markets come alive with hawkers vending their goods to bargaining grandmothers, shops flaunting their billowing sales to employees whose wallets are full, from a bonus in the salary and of course the chattering of children as they whine for a chocolate ice-cream instead of a lemon one. The pleasing smell of crisp *dosas* cooking in every alley and nook you turn to, acts as a dose of heaven for foodies like me. The busy evenings spent in market-hopping are quite enjoyable. Roaming in the famous Jayanagar market buzzing with chatter and *kappi* (filter coffee) is an exhilarating experience. My personal favourite *dosa* shop is dose camp that sells awesome *dosas* right off the tawa onto our banana leaf with a cube of *desi ghee* melting away to glory on top just like the cherry on the cake! Seeing woks steaming with piping hot veg manchurian in every *darshini* we pass by is mouth-watering. But the greatest experience during the trip is the variety of shops that we see in the markets selling such colourful pants, shirts, handkerchiefs and what not! The delicacies of Bengaluru are in complete contrast from the ones I enjoy in Lucknow! My favourite is *masalapoori*. Crunchy *pooris* and juicy pea curry topped with *sev* and chutney! Aha! Its heaven on the taste buds. But the highlight of the entire trip is the visit to *Ajja's* (maternal grandfather) home.

Despite there being so many scenic locations in and around Bengaluru my heart swells with the vibrant hues and colours of sheer cheer as I anticipate the warmth and comfort in my dearest grandparents' mansion. Although it might be a little small it is larger than a palace from my point of view. My favourite things about my grandparents' house are the many stationery and magazine shops around it. A shop full of comic books is just a jump away and the art supplies shop is a trot away from *Ajja's* home. The neighbourhood shopkeepers there also crack many jokes with me and make me laugh till I tear up. A supermarket by the name MK Ahmed is full of everything a household needs but the third floor is paradise for me. A variety of special edition Uniball pens, exciting activity books, cute canvases, and easels and what not! The shop is amazing. What's more? It is just a minute's walk from *Ajji's* house. it feels as though I, as a pirate, have embarked on a treasure hunt in *Ajja's* house whose prize would be a daring raid on the snacks in the kitchen. The sailor would have infinite powers in the form of *Ajja's* love and no weaknesses in the form of *Ajji's* care! And then this would be an epic voyage … in *Ajja's* sea! I always anticipate the never dying joy and excitement in *Ajja's* eyes as he greets me with a hug each time I visit him. The days I have spent enjoying a healthy regular lifestyle with my *Ajja* are those that are embedded in my memory. My *Ajja* inspires me to keep working hard and strive harder for my goal. He wakes up early in the morning and goes out to buy the groceries irrespective of his health or knee pain. He has a regular routine that he keenly follows. Watching tv soaps and IPL matches with my dearest *Ajja* while relaxing on his buoyant tummy is indeed refreshing. Hearing children, parents, workers, colleagues, and most importantly my *Ajja – Ajji* speak my mother tongue: Kannada is music to my ears.

My sweet *Ajji* always prepares my favourite rice and *poha papads*, whenever I stay with her. The delicious *rasam* and *sambhar* that *Ajji* makes for me are unparalleled in the world. My *Ajji* is so intent on keeping her surroundings clean that I feel ashamed if I make one of the rooms untidy. She believes in not being dependent on anyone and rather does all the housework herself without any house help. Her determination is indeed motivational.

No visit to Bengaluru is complete without a visit to my beloved brother's place – Skanda. The many hours spent playing with him and secretly planning pranks on a sleepy afternoon are unforgettable. I cannot convey the immeasurable joy that I experience on being sent with him to purchase chips and groceries to the neighbouring shops. It is Skanda's presence at Ajja's house that makes the trip one that is close to my heart. From exchanging amazing tales from school to hours of trying to cheat each other at Ludo these countless memories shall forever be cherished by me. It is a delight to visit my *Dadi's* house in the City of Gardens and enjoy her home-made *kadabu* along with spending leisure's hours with her listening to my father's childhood stories.

Being the only granddaughter, it is a memorable experience getting pampered generously by *Dadi*.

Visiting cousins and relatives, enjoying their fond hospitality, and giving small gifts to them are some exciting trips during my stay at Bengaluru, whenever I arrive at my grandparents' magnificent abode. The trip to Bengaluru is always an exciting tour to make as I constantly await the fun and joy at my grandparents' home. It is the emotional connection to the IT hub that attracts me there. The infinite love showered upon me, the fun games I play, and of course spending quality time with my *Ajja* and *Ajji* are the things that pull me closer to my hometown year after year.

7

A Second Call To The Mountains - Trek To Kuari Pass

The excitement in my voice rose as I came to know that I was to go on another trek after a gap of three years, the previous one being Dayara Bugyal.

The experience of being in the mountains once again has added another feather of memories to my hat, and here I will share my experience of going to the Kuari Pass Trek in March 2022.

On the 20th of March we reached Tapovan, our basecamp, from Rishikesh. The previous day, I had an exciting flight all the way from Lucknow to Dehradun. The next day we had a rather long but mesmerising trip from Rishikesh to Tapovan. After a short introduction with the guides- Laxman Uncle, Anil Bhaiyya and Trek Leader Parthy Sir, we retired to our rooms.

The next day we started our trek, which was very tedious and reminded me of my most tiring days. It was a difficult day as we had to acclimatize properly and the trail was dusty and dry leaves and twigs crackled under our feet as we treaded on them and in places the lush green grass felt soft and mushy.

With steep ascent and frequent encounter with beautiful trees along with the wonderful stories about Uttarakhand and nature from Anil Bhaiyya we finally reached the best campsite that I had ever been to –Akhrotghetta.

At Akhrotghetta, our tent was located just beside the famous walnut tree with the wonderful view of the mountain peaks - Hathi-Ghoda, Rishikund and Dronagiri.

That afternoon, I went walnut hunting and found many in their shells but many of them were charred. While telling my experience and discovery to my mother I entered our tent and put my walnuts into a bag.

The following day, we woke up early and were able to witness the beautiful sunrise over the Himalayas sipping the refreshing black tea. I bid goodbye to Akhrotghetta and the tiny stream which gurgled joyfully and lulled me to sleep at night.

On the second day of our trek which was fairly easy, we spotted patches of snow! On the way to our second campsite Khullara we paid our respects to Lord Ganpati at a tiny temple. We finally reached a rather overcrowded Khullara and had a filling lunch. There it was very windy and colder than Akhrotghetta, so we were always packed in warm jackets and sweaters. In the night, the temperature went down to -5 or -6 degrees.

When I came to know that I was to climb the summit the next day, I was very excited and had a deep sleep dreaming all about playing and sliding in the snow. We woke up around 4:30 AM in the morning so that we could start our trek for the summit day early.

The temperature was -0.1 degrees when we had started to walk on snow.

Throughout the day's trek we had to tread through the snow. I trekked along with a lot of enthusiasm although at times, I nearly lost hope of reaching the summit. The scariest part was around a corner where many boulders with melting snow on them and a cliff on the other side, but thankfully with the help of Anil Bhaiyya I could cross the section with ease.

When I finally reached the summit, I triumphantly pranced around with a piece of chocolate promised by Harshil Bhaiyya (one of the trekkers). Everyone praised me for being able to conquer the summit of Kuari Pass at the age of eleven.

After enjoying the view of 32 peaks, clicking many photos and hearing the story from Anil Bhaiyya on why the trek was named Lord Curzon's Trail and Kuari Pass we started to descend down . At a particular point, I started to slide down and it was rather fun but, in the end, I always used to slide down like a ball on a slide.

When we were nearing the campsite an almost 90-degree descent section came where Anil Bhai went to help my mother. There I decided to rest and sat on the nearby tree trunk, but uh-oh! As soon as I sat on it, I tumbled headfirst and momentarily was totally upside-down. I was so stunned that I remained in the same position for a few seconds.

Regaining my balance, I stood up carefully and sat on the cold rock-like snow beside me and waited for a while. The coolness of the snow was pretty soothing to my aching thighs. After a short while my father came and we both started to descend down further. Then again, I slipped on ice and cried in pain. Finally, when we could see Khullara, I felt a new surge of energy and relief in my body and rather energetically started to descend down.

After reaching Khullara I sensed a feeling of accomplishment of reaching the height of 12,516 feet successfully. That afternoon it snowed slightly but my joy knew no bounds to be able to see the snowfall and the snow.

Later that evening in the dining tent we watched the '14 Peaks' movie halfway through. After a sound sleep that night, we woke up nice and fresh the next morning. With a hearty breakfast we started to descend down towards Karchi village. Laxman Uncle took me shortcut by shortcut and thus I reached the village first. Raksh Bhaiyya (one of the trekkers) clicked many photos of mine. After a short drive to Joshimath we had our lunch and went to our dorms. The following morning, we started our journey back home.

On the way back home, I was reflecting back on my experience of the trek I realised that I had learnt a lot of things, like- being independent, being physically and mentally fit for any challenge in life, being determined & having a never-give-up spirit, being more social, adjusting with others and many more.

The sight from the Kuari Pass summit will always remain in my heart. This trek has proved to me that the mountains will keep calling me time and again and I will keep doing more treks in the future.

Hope that the next call comes soon...

8

Off to the Reader's Paradise

The beautiful memories of the unforgettable trip to the nation's hub of all activities: New Delhi, in 2023, flooded back to me as I stepped down from the Lucknow Mail. My mind was chuffing with new exciting thoughts about my impending visit to the World Book Fair, at Pragati Maidan the next day.

I remember myself gazing as I saw the Red Fort, India Gate, Jantar Mantar and other such national monuments loom in front of me the previous year. This year also, I was looking forward to the weekend in the nation's capital.

The sun was smiling down at us, spreading its golden rays as the sky turned a pale lavender bidding the day farewell and allowing the night to draw on at the bustling railway station. I jumped with joy and anticipation for the upcoming excitement, the next two days. Finally, we were off to the nation's centre: New Delhi.

I was off to a voracious reader's heaven, the famous World Book Fair at Pragati Maidan to present my second book 'The Epic Storymania'. As the morning rays shone in from the adjacent train window, I rubbed my eyes open to see beautiful mustard fields rolling past and cows mooing good morning to us. After such a pleasant start to the day, soon we left for Pragati Maidan via metro. Ah! The scenes from the metro were mesmerizing. It felt amazing to catch glimpses of the high-rise buildings before they sped into the horizon as the metro train zoomed to its next station. Finally, when we arrived at Pragati Maidan, I was taken in by the mighty building of the Supreme Court towering on one side and the renowned World Book Fair buzzing with activity on the other.

Once inside the book fair, it felt as though I would lose myself inside it. It was that huge! There were stalls and stalls of books and I just stood rooted to the spot staring at them until my father thumped me on the back to keep moving. I felt as though my dearest companions, my books, had thrown a great grand party to welcome me to Delhi. We casually walked around looking at all the book stalls and finally found the publishing house we were looking for in the World Book Fair - 'Notion Press' stall. I was delighted to get an opportunity to present my book at one of India's largest publishers. My heart was skipping with happiness. I was given a memento badge as I was one of the youngest authors there for that day. After an engaging live interview with the enthusiastic interviewer there I left with a wide, pompous grin pasted on my face. After a filling lunch we strolled on in the fair, entering various stalls, buying several books, and of course fulfilling our literary cravings. As a connoisseur of English, this visit to the fair was a treasure trove for me indeed. It was an encouragement for me to keep writing and leave an indelible mark in the world of literature. Some of my favourite stalls at the World Book Fair were Penguin Publishing House, Rupa Publications, CBT Publications, NBT Publications etc. The experience was made even special with valuable insights on a wide variety of books from fellow booklovers who seeing my interest as I sifted through the vast volumes, shared with me their experiences of reading specific books and suggested their favourites for me to read. After enjoying ourselves to the fullest we ambled along to the legendary Sarojini Nagar Market where we shopped and shopped till we dropped! We pushed our cramp feet a few metres more to our all-time favourite restaurant – Haldiram's. We stuffed ourselves with the delicious Delhi cuisine until we could eat no more.

The next morning, after a deep sleep we woke up fresh and pondered on how to spend the day before we left for Lucknow again. My mother suggested a *darshan* of Akshardham. We liked the idea and at once left for the holy temple. After waiting for quite some time, we entered the temple and my goodness! Never have I ever seen such beautiful intricate carvings on sandstone or marble! The domes in each part of the temple had a unique interesting design. I could not take my eyes off the beautiful elephants sculpted in sandstone. The shawls draped on each elephant had a distinctive design, even every fold and crease on the shawl was shaped by the sculptors carefully to make it appear life-like. After satisfying our taste buds with the eminent Gujarati cuisine available at Akshardham we started our way back to our dear city, Lucknow again.

As we waited patiently on the railway platform for The

Tejas to arrive, I reflected on the entire trip to New Delhi. I recalled the feeling of my heart skipping a few beats as I stepped into the Eden for all readers: The World Book Fair! I can never forget the exhilaration I experienced as I answered the questions promptly during the interview at the Notion Press Stall. Suddenly the hoot of an approaching train broke my reverie and I hastened to pick up my bags and board the train. As the Tejas thundered to the platform, I admired its sleek yellow and orange exterior, its smooth rolling wheels and shining engine. It was indeed an exciting experience to travel aboard a superfast train. As the train sped along, evening turned to twilight and finally the night fell. We enjoyed the amazing journey to the fullest. Finally, after a thrilling trip we returned to our dearest City of Nawabs: Lucknow! It was a special feeling as I felt the familiar buzz of the Charbagh Railway Station envelop me as I stepped down from the train to leave for a journey back home.

9

How the Chattisgarh Jungle Trek left me stunned

My eyes glimmered and twinkled with joy when I came to know that we were going on another trek after a gap of just a few months after triumphing the summit of the Kuari Pass Trek.

I recollect my memories of the trek, my pencil to pen down my experience at the enrapturing Chhattisgarh Jungle Trek.

I clearly remember the happy smile that made its way to a broad grin on my face on the first day of the trek. On the 22nd of December we drove all the way from Baikunthpur to Ramgarh before which we had flown from Lucknow to Raipur and boarded the Durg-Ambikapur Express to reach Baikunthpur. After a short introduction with our trek leader- Ashish sir and guide Suhkram ji, we packed our lunch and went into a forest clearing for briefing. Post that, we trekked along on dry, crackling, leafy paths and saw a large number of pugmarks even those of a bear! But what stole the spotlight for the day for me was the rock climbing! I climbed the rock with great vigour and excitement but soon felt helpless at a particular point but Ashish sir encouraged me on and I was finally able to overcome the zenith of the rock! When I reached the pinnacle of the rock, I felt like I could queen over the whole world. To celebrate my victory, after reaching the top, I distributed some of the toffees I had in my waist pouch to the other co–trekkers who shared the victory of reaching the peak of the rock with me. That day, we really and truly lived through 'Jungle Book' as we explored the cave where Mowgli was brought up in, in the story by Rudyard Kipling. We then descended and trekked on to reach our very first campsite Turripani - a small tribal mud hut that was coated with cow dung all over. It was a unique experience for me to spend the night in the mud hut with the cool night air and the sound of swaying branches of the leafy trees that stood sheltering the hut lulling me to sleep.

The next morning, pride and happiness rippled through my veins when I was made the trek leader for the day! I led the team very enthusiastically although at times I deviated from the right trail; Sukhram ji was always there to guide me. It was a relatively shorter day, but we all were very tired as the sun was beating down hard on us but all our hard work was rewarded when we came to the most picturesque campsite of all the treks that I have ever done – Tadiyabaan. I got the best tent with the most scenic view of the Tadiya lake. That night as I lay in my sleeping bag waiting for sleep to come over me, I chuckled to myself as I pondered happily over the nickname some of my amiable co–trekkers had given me – THE CAPTAIN. Ashish sir had even decided to stick a small piece of tape with my nickname on my coffee mug! But as these thoughts revolved in my curious mind my eyes started drooping and I had fallen into a deep slumber.

The following morning, we all set off on the longest leg of our trek – to Pandupara. We packed 2 rolls of chapatti each as lunch and moved on. On the trail, I was having a conversation with the star photographer of our team, Amit bhaiya, fun-loving Anusha didi and humorous Ananth bhaiya about their favourite things. We stopped under a cluster of trees to have lunch accompanied by a beautiful view. As we all munched on our rolls, we cherished the last evening's memory, where we had experienced the most beautiful sunset ever over the Tadiya lake. There we had clicked loads of pictures and made it a sweet memory. I had sipped my favourite black tea as I sat beside Sandhya didi seeing the sun disappear below the horizon and the night rolling in. Unknowingly Amit bhaiya recorded us chattering away with the glamorous sunset in the backdrop. The other co-trekkers were discussing the last evening's scary tales and incidents in various treks told by Ashish sir with red light shining on his face. But soon we made a move to the most rewarding campsite of all - Pandupura. The last kilometre we had to walk in the Gopat river. As soon as I put my foot in, a refreshed feeling pulsed through me, and I began splashing about in the cool water with immense joy. We ran in the water spraying it all around. I felt like I was not at all tired and was having the time of my life. I jumped and splashed about to my heart's content even after reaching the campsite. My favourite spot was where the water fell on a rock and the current was high and soothing. I stood there fearlessly with only the rocks to support me, astounding Anusha didi, Ananth bhaiya and Avinash bhaiya. But then we had to get back to the campsite. More excitingly, that night, around a bonfire or rather a safety fire to drive away animals as I would call it, we sat down to listen to some interesting incidents by our teammates with rapt attention. The fire was creating a warm glow on everyone's face. After a delicious dinner we slept off in a happy mood.

The next morning, with my eyes shining with joy I jumped into the water with great relish. Soon the child in everyone came out and they began pushing each other into the water playfully. We enjoyed ourselves to the fullest that day. I got too wet and cold while playing so Arjun bhaiya lent me one of his T-shirts very kindly and Anusha didi generously helped me to change. But nevertheless, I played in the water to my heart's content. If this was not enough, we drove to Ramgarh in an open pick-up truck with all of us hooting and hollering with joy. After a hot lunch we settled down de-briefing. It was nice to listen to everyone's experiences and even better to receive a memorable magnet. This was an enchantingly different trek for me. I loved this trek, my co trekkers' and trek leader's friendly spirit.

That evening, as I slept in the Durg–Ambikapur express, I reflected over the valuable lessons this trek taught me-

I learnt to socialize and adjust with various people of different age-groups and walks of life and also learnt how to sustain myself minimalistically, became increasingly independent and acquired the quality of being grateful to people who helped me. Most importantly, I learnt how to make good friends, whom I can trust to help me in the time of need, just like most of my co-trekkers. People do voice the truth when they say that 'Nature is the best Teacher.'

The diversity of the splendour of India has stunned me so much that I earnestly hope nature will invite me soon to experience its beauty once again.

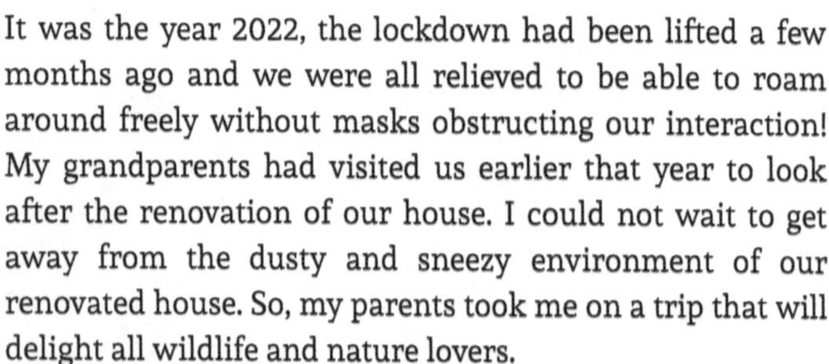

10

Into the forests of the northeast

It was the year 2022, the lockdown had been lifted a few months ago and we were all relieved to be able to roam around freely without masks obstructing our interaction! My grandparents had visited us earlier that year to look after the renovation of our house. I could not wait to get away from the dusty and sneezy environment of our renovated house. So, my parents took me on a trip that will delight all wildlife and nature lovers.

As the airplane soared in the sky, my heart too flew up in high hopes as we flew to the unexplored natural paradise of India: The Northeast. Every cell of my body jumped up in excitement as the aircraft landed on the runway in Bagdogra. I was very excited to finally be able to relax on a holiday trip with my parents. It was delightful that I would be able to savour the rich culture, scenic beauty, the varying cuisine and most importantly the mesmerizing Buddhist monasteries and gompas of the Northeast. The road twisted up the hills and slid down the knolls in circles as our car made its way to Sikkim's grand hilly capital: Gangtok. The scenery was astounding. My eyes were on the verge of popping out of their sockets when I saw the spell-binding greenery around us. As our car neared the pretty capital of Sikkim, the sky started darkening as the sun bid us goodbye for the day and the mighty moon rose up to let the night flourish in her milky light. Finally, after sitting in the car for hours on end, seeing the hills roll into the scenery while the others scuttled away to make space for the next; we finally reached our cosy hotel by the name 'Sikkim Retreat'. Our lodge was located along a curve, such that one could catch a glimpse of the beautiful mountains that loomed large in the background whenever one looked out of the window. We were happily exhausted from the long day, thus after a quick dinner we hustled to bed. The following morning was spent in sightseeing the picturesque city of Gangtok where we saw the temples of Ganesh Tok and Hanuman Tok along with the eye-catching Tashi View Point where we were able to spot the mighty Kanchenjunga Peak. Never in my life will I ever forget the exhilarating experience on the first day of our trip when I did ziplining for the first time in my life! Rain was pounding hard on the windscreen of the cab, I was hesitant to try this adventure sport in the volley of water over the gushing Bakthang Falls but realized that this was a once-in-a-lifetime opportunity, so I willed myself to climb the slippery rocks to attempt something thrilling and dangerous. As they lightly pushed me off the chair to zipline across the deep abyss below, I screamed in fear for a moment but then at the very next moment started giggling in joy as I enjoyed the stimulating ride across the waterfall. As the experience ended I started wondering why I was so uncertain to try such a sport a few minutes ago. As our car rumbled on to the National Institute of Tibetology Museum my mind wandered to the visit to an emporium where there were many souvenirs among which I purchased an adorable hand-made Red Panda Keychain as a memento of my visit to the red panda's home: Sikkim. On reaching the Tibetology Museum we saw many palm-leaf manuscripts of the olden times. Our day ended with a peaceful ride in the Gangtok Ropeway and a visit to the iconic MG Marg in the city. I still remember the delight filling my lungs as our car wove its way up the mountain all the way to Tsongo Lake at 12,400 feet passing by a stunning waterfall and breath-taking hills. Soon, enveloped by a curtain of water we were at the Nathula Pass (Indo-China border) at 14,500 feet with eyes popping in amazement as the timings on mobile phones showed dual times, that is Indian and Chinese time both! My chest swelled in pride for my nation. I was on cloud nine on being able to cross out the second border off my list with the first one being the Indo-Pak border in Punjab. I was even happier that I received a certificate confirming my visit to Nathula Pass from Indian Army soldiers. But what stole the spotlight that day was the visit to the Lal Bazaar. The shopping spree there marked the end of a pleasurable stay in the Land of Monasteries: Gangtok.

I can never forget the three days we spent in Tinchulay. The place was built in the middle of a quaint forest! On the way to the beautiful homestay, we came across a gurgling river gushing from a great height that was worth a ton of pictures. My heart jumped in joy as we drove on, passing the scenic hills. As our car climbed laboriously up the steep cobbled path I caught a glimpse of the impressive Kanchenjunga peak. Even before I could yelp in surprise, the summit hid itself again behind the snug blanket of clouds. The homestay was magnificent! It was built in the traditional style of construction, made entirely with wood. The best part of the experience was that we had two cute dogs for company throughout our stay. As the place was surrounded by dense woods, we embarked on a short exploratory trip to it. There we saw such a stunning variety of plants and trees, ferns and moss and what not! But the encounter was a little bit painful as well for many leeches took a liking to our feet and decided to have a taste of our Lucknowi blood. The high point of the entire trip was the spell binding tea estate that was on the way to the mesmerizing Lamahatta Eco Park near Tinchulay. There we saw a vast stretch of pine, dhupi and large cardamom trees along with the looming Mount Kanchenjunga. My father and I saw a picturesque lake after hiking up for a kilometre in the park. We enjoyed ourselves to the fullest. The following morning, we went to the charming little town of Kalimpong. It was full of beautiful gardens. My mind could not stop wondering if I had accidently landed in a foreign country, it was so picture-perfect! The hills and knolls were the perfect shade of green, the crown of the trees was so seamlessly round as though a beautiful scenery from one of my watercolour paintings had come alive to delight me. There was a slight nip in the air that sent a pleasant shiver down the spine. Our visit to the Delo Park won my heart as I enjoyed its tour, riding a sweet white horse. We even visited the interesting Kalimpong Science Centre. There were many experiential learning experiments through which we were able to understand the simple concepts of physics. But the day was edged with sadness as well for we had to unwillingly leave our favourite location to embark on the journey to the last location on our travel plan: Darjeeling, 'the queen of the hills'. Oh! I almost forgot! If we did not buy tea from the Northeast then our trip would remain incomplete, wouldn't it? So, my family and I bought so many packets of tea that a funny thought popped into my mind, saying that we could export this Darjeeling tea to England personally in our Nano and make some good money! Ha-ha! On the way to the mesmerising hill station of Darjeeling we visited the Padmaja Naidu Himalayan Zoological Park & Himalayan Mountaineering Institute. It was awesome! We saw a cute red panda dangling from the branches yearning for attention, an elegant tiger flaunting his stripes, a swift leopard jumping from branch to branch and a pair of black bears having a fun fight session. I thoroughly enjoyed myself at the adventure setup for children at the Himalayan Mountaineering Institute. Never have I ever felt such intense thrill or joy in my life that left every cell in my body trembling in excitement. Stepping over the colourful tyres, crawling through the tin tunnel all dangling from a few sturdy trees to a sheer drop below. The beautiful Batase Loop shall always remain embedded in my memory as that evening my mother's camera captured my photos dressed up in a traditional Sikkimese attire! That day as we sat in our cab going back to the hotel, watching the torrent of water gushing on the windscreen, I wondered if the children there even had to fill their water bottles at home or not! All they had to do was dangle their bottle out of the kitchen window and ta-da! Their flask would be filled! The sight of the Kanchenjunga at the Tiger Hill got firmly entrenched in my mind as I stood there in awe, gazing at the mountain. My mother and I enjoyed a fine shopping spree at the Mall Road, and the Chowk Market on the two days we spent in Darjeeling. The sun smiled down at me as I chuckled in joy as we enjoyed a joyous trip aboard one of the sweetest heritage trains in India: The

Toy Train! The engine pulled the two coaches along as my father, mother and I smiled goofily getting pictures clicked with the mesmerizing background slightly obscured by the steam of the Darjeeling Himalayan Railway. The mighty Himalayas towered to the left while the right side was covered with rocky cliffs. It was a mind-boggling experience! The highlight of the entire train journey was the visit to India's highest railway station: Ghum railway station! The rail museum there was so exciting! There were so many ancient engines and coaches there that I was on the verge of hopping into the cockpit of the engine with a bottle of diesel in my hand and becoming India's youngest train engine driver! After the enjoyable time spent in the Toy Train we left to gain some inner 'peace' at the Peace Pagoda. The platinum white exterior dotted with colourful splashes was indeed a sight to behold. My heart felt much more at peace while at the Pagoda. My heart had to resist the temptation of abandoning everything right there and then and becoming an ascetic chanting *om mani padme hum* until Lord Buddha himself came to escort me to *nirvana*!

Well, it had been indeed a lovely experience, exploring the unexplored, seeing the unseen and hearing the unheard. This encounter with the diversity of the Northeast shall forever be embedded in my heart. The feel of the icy mountain air on my cheeks has made a space for itself in my heart. The walks in the buzzing markets of Gangtok are unforgettable! The tranquil forests of Tinchulay helped us calm our nerves as nature soothed us with her spell-binding beauty. The bazaars of Darjeeling were full of hustle and bustle that reminded me of the crowd at Aminabad in Lucknow. The hoot of the Toy Train as it sped on its tracks brings a pleasant smile to my face whenever I think of it. This trip was full of fun, food, culture, and rumbling clouds! It was a once-in-a-lifetime experience that I can never forget. The Northeast was a new face of India which I had never seen before. Tata!

11

Adventuring into the wild on my Own

As I poise my pencil over the paper, I recollect the memories of this beautiful trekking summer camp to the Deorital-Chandrashila Trek which gave me the feeling of pleasure, adventure, and independence I had been craving for months.

I remember my heart thumping with excitement as I waved my parents goodbye at the Live Free Hostel to go on another trek just five to six months after completing the mesmerizing Chhattisgarh Jungle Trek, that too, this time all alone! Seeing the hills roll past, an odd tree or two peeping out during the enjoyable drive to the base camp, Sari. I felt like a bird who had set sail on its life's most eventful journey.

On reaching Sari, we met Mowgli, a lively young dog who accompanied us throughout the trek along with two other canines. After a brief introductory session where we were told about our trek leader– Tina ma'am, our guides– Bijju bhaiya and Anup bhaiya, and last but not least, our interns– Srushti, Panchami, Sri bhaiya, Aritra sir, and Abhishek sir. We then packed our backpacks for the next day's trek and slept with great expectations for the first day of trekking scuttling in our minds.

The following morning saw me trekking up stony paths where grassy clearings seemed a relief. As we relaxed near the Deoriatal Lake I gazed at the pink algae-like things floating around, happy tadpoles skirting the edges of the lake, dense forests on three sides and an effortlessly rolling bugyal in front made me realize that I had become more resilient and even bolder. We soon reached our stunning campsite– Deoriatal.

That evening while we played fun games in the dining tent a strong gale began blowing and the tents were on the verge of flying off. We enjoyed ourselves thoroughly at the campsite marvelling at the beauty of the mesmerizing Deoriatal lake from the viewpoint.

The next day we were laughing and smiling as we made our way through beautiful rhododendron forests where we even ate its tangy red flowers, to the most extensive campsite I have ever seen– Syalmi. My eyes were attracted to the greenery around Syalmi and I liked it at once. I was amazed to see that I had withstood the test of strength and willpower as I climbed the Jhandi Top and Rohini Bugyal. That night as we stargazed, I spotted a group of foxes staring at us with their nocturnal eyes shining.

The following morning, I woke up early to see the first rays of the sun hit the snow-capped peaks and they turned a faint lilac pink, my favorite color. The entire day was spent completing adventurous tasks and learning survival skills with our team led by Aritra sir. All the activities were successfully completed under our team's pilots, Tarush bhaiya and Swapnil bhaiya.

That day we also celebrated the birthday of our new friend– Vaidehi, right after Sri Bhaiya's epic snakebite act.

That night as I slept snugly in my sleeping bag, I went over my experiences which included how to remain calm in times of crisis as well as some new survival skills like pitching a tent out of only a groundsheet and trek poles.

The following day, before leaving, we unpitched our tents and drew hilarious portraits of each other where I added an extremely funny element to my best friend– Soha's portrait. I trekked energetically and went to the Akashkamini River where I felt utter calm on feeling the current of the cold water hitting my legs.

I comprehended that I had bonded better with nature by now and walked on to reach our campsite, Baniya Kund. After lunch, we were asked to pitch our tents on our own which was an exciting experience altogether as we pushed in the rods and made our tent perfectly. Then we had the summit briefing. My tentmate - Soha and I, packed our daypacks for the grand day as we chatted about it endlessly. We even made a checklist of items to ensure that we didn't leave anything out. That night we set off for the Chandrashila summit at 1AM! We trekked excitedly, flashing headlights that few of our friends mistook to be the eyes of wolves. We pulled up our socks and bucked up for the final summit push! As I pushed myself on, Sri bhaiya kept encouraging me to climb on. I felt a sense of great achievement when I finally triumphed at the Summit in time.

We danced around celebrating our victory and witnessing a cloudy sunrise. As we all sat down on the rocks, I gazed at the mighty snowy Mount Chaukhamba rising high into the clouds. It seemed a hand's length away and seeing a seven-thousand-meter mountain up close was an incredible experience for me. It instilled an aspiration in me to touch new heights and reach my goal.

As we descended, we stopped at the beautiful Tungnath Temple for darshan. As I stood in front of the deity, praying I hoped that my mother was with me as she would love the experience. I also remembered my grandfather and wished to tell him that I had visited one of the highest Shiva temples in the world. Later we took a break at a dhaba for a second round of breakfast of scrumptious aloo paratha.

On the way down, I was cracking jokes with Ayam and Shachi, the Slope Manager of the trek. On returning to Baniya Kund most of us rested because we were tired. In the evening we celebrated our friend Arundhati's birthday. Later we exchanged our summit experiences as we sat in a group. I completed my Trek Memory Booklet where everyone wrote a couple of qualities of mine. The one which delighted me the most was Tina Ma'am's expression of me being independent.

The next morning before leaving for Sari, Tina Ma'am took our debriefing session where everyone expressed their unique reflections and takeaways from the entire trek. I shared my own learnings as I had a wonderful experience. I would try to reduce waste generation at home and take home a lot of values I had picked up from everyone. Then we journeyed in the Tempo Traveller to Sari.

Once everyone got their smartphones back at Sari, they contacted their family but I was a bit sad. Seeing my sad face Tina ma'am let me talk to my parents with her mobile phone. I was overjoyed and thanked her profusely. I had missed my mother a lot as I was so far away from her for so long for the first time but it also made me realize how dependent I was on her.

As we drove back to Rishikesh through the winding roads and enchanting scenery I reflected on my learnings from the trek. I realized that now I knew to handle myself better and adapt easily to the environment around me. Now I am a more independent girl who knows how to make her friends. I was joyous to meet my parents in Rishikesh but also sad to say goodbye to my new friends. As our train ambled onto my dear Lucknow, I recollected the experiences of my four treks and how I had grown into a confident and experienced trekker. This trek will always occupy a special place in my heart as it was my very first trek without my parents and I want to have more treks as feathers in my hat. And now here I am, penning my experience to share it with the world.

12

Signing off with a Traveler's Stamp

This collection of travelogues holds a special place in my heart. It is a testament to my joy of travelling, of exploring the world with my very own eyes and marking my presence there with my footprints. Each view, each scene evoked a piece of prose and poetry in my mind. Every voyage into the deep, mesmerizing sea of this beautiful world has been exhilarating, exciting and relaxing.

I have always had a dream of visiting all the cities and states of my exquisite nation. It is a wish that is being fulfilled part by part, year by year. I have visited the eight corners of India- The Himalayas in the North; Assam, Sikkim and West Bengal in the Northeast, Odisha in the East, Puducherry in the Southeast, Bengaluru in the Southwest, Gujarat in the West and Rajasthan in the Northwest apart from many, many other places. But you see, out of the 28 states of my country, some are still standing in line to join my musty corner of travel chronicles. This line is quite long but in the upcoming years it will become shorter by tenfold.

I hope this book has been a joyful read for you. Exploring and travelling is an emotion for me and for all those who helped me bring my dream of travelling and writing to reality, including – my beloved mother and father. Finally, I conclude by saying, I believe reading books is a delight but writing stories for others to enjoy is an even greater pleasure. So,

Happy Reading!
Happy exploring!
Toodles till next time!